CLEAN YOUR HEART

PEACE COUSCIOUSNESS AND PROGRAMS

ShanYuPing Jiang

Clean Your Heart
Peace Cousciousness and Programs

Copyright © 2022 by ShanYuPing Jiang.

Paperback ISBN: 978-1-63812-222-7
Hardcover ISBN: 978-1-63812-232-6
Ebook ISBN: 978-1-63812-223-4

All rights reserved. No part in this book may be produced and transmitted in any form or by any means, electronic, or mechanical, including photocopying, recording, or by any information storage and retrieval system, without permission in writing from the copyright owner.

The views expressed in this work are solely those of the author and do not necessarily reflect the views of the publisher hereby disclaims any responsibility for them.

Published by Pen Culture Solutions   03/28/2022

Pen Culture Solutions
1-888-727-7204 (USA)
1-800-950-458 (Australia)
support@penculturesolutions.com

Introduction

This book is intended to Enlighten people. Human consciousness is like a computer system, and the faith system is the foundation program for sustaining the whole system.

Truth is like a bug to smash all programs. When the bug makes the whole system break down, enlightenment is reached. There will be a non-system human.

When one person unloads the system, wisdom may appear.

If you require milk, you need a glass.

This system is a constraint. When people free themselves from it, they become who they naturally are. The process may be a little uncomfortable because people still think they are the system itself.

This book includes several courses which need to be copied by handwriting or typing. It doesn't matter whether people think or not; this material is processed in the subconscious.

Course 1

Are there really eyeballs? Why is it not the information from touch and images that returns to the brain and then is perceived? Why not? Why no?

Are there really noses? Why is it not the information from touch and images that returns to the brain and then is perceived? Why not? Why no?

Are there really mouths? Why is it not the information from touch and images that returns to the brain and then is perceived? Why not? Why no?

Are there really ears? Why is it not the information from touch, voice, and images that returns to the brain and then is perceived? Why not? Why no?

Are there really tongues? Why is it not the information from touch and images that returns to the brain and then is perceived? Why not? Why no?

You may use them every day, but do you know what they really are?

Stay piece and alone.

The first course helps people thinks through five senses. Humans connect this world through five senses, make effort through five senses. It is the persistence to five senses which makes one person believe that the authenticity of everything.

Course 1 requires a handwriting or typing. It is not that important for one to think how the course processing in one's mind. The course processing in one's subconscious. Once finish the course, the feeling back inside will be altered. It is the persistence of one's ego block the inner peace. This peace leads to mental relaxation and freedom.

Course 2

Is anxiety real? Why is it not the information from scent, touch, voice, taste, and images that returns to the brain and then triggers the program in the brain, or it operates automatically, and then is perceived? Why not? Why no?

Is uneasy real? Why is it not the information from scent, touch, voice, taste, and images that returns to the brain and then triggers the program in the brain, or it operates automatically, and then is perceived? Why not? Why no?

Is fear real? Why is it not the information from scent, touch, voice, taste, and images that returns to the brain and then triggers the program in the brain, or it operates automatically, and then is perceived? Why not? Why no?

Is anger real? Why is it not the information from scent, touch, voice, taste, and images that returns to the brain and then triggers the program in the brain, or it operates automatically, and then is perceived? Why not? Why no?

Is pride real? Why is it not the information from scent, touch, voice, taste, and images that returns to the brain and then triggers the program in the brain, or it operates automatically, and then is perceived? Why not? Why no?

Emotions are always taking control of us. What if they are just a collection of programs?

Course 2 relieves one's persistence of emotions. Persistence of both rationality and sensibility blocks the inner peace. Neither rationality or sensibility cannot lead to inner peace.

Course 3

Is the body real? Why is it not the information from scent, touch, voice, taste, and images that returns to the brain and then is perceived? Why not? Why no?

Is the brain real? Why is it not the information from scent, touch, voice, taste, and images that returns to the brain and then is perceived? Why not? Why no?

Am I real? Why is it not the information from scent, touch, voice, taste, and images that returns to the brain, creating various ideas, and then is perceived? Why not? Why no?

Is despair real? Why is it not the information from scent, touch, voice, taste, and images that returns to the brain and then triggers the program in the brain, or it operates automatically, and then is perceived? Why not? Why no?

Are friends real? Why is it not the information from scent, touch, voice, taste, and images that returns to the brain and then is perceived? Why not? Why no?

You can ask yourself similar questions.

The persistence of body or kinds of feelings also block the inner peace. Course 3 requires to relief the persistence of body and feelings, it is not requires one to harm their body. Please do love your body and takes good care of health.

Course 4

Is family real? Why is it not the information from scent, touch, voice, taste, and images that returns to the brain and then is perceived? Why not? Why no?

Is Buddha real? Why is it not the information from scent, touch, voice, and images that returns to the brain and then is perceived? Why not? Why no?

Is Jesus real? Why is it not the information from scent, touch, voice, taste, and images that returns to the brain and then is perceived? Why not? Why no?

Is Muhammad real? Why is it not the information of scent, touch, voice, taste, and images that returns to the brain and then is perceived? Why not? Why no?

Is God real? Why is it not the information from scent, touch, voice, taste, and images that returns to the brain and then is perceived? Why not? Why no?

Is Allah real? Why is it not the information from scent, touch, voice, taste, and images that returns to the brain and then is perceived? Why not? Why no?

Is Siva real? Why is it not the information from scent, touch, voice, taste, and images that returns to the brain and then is perceived? Why not? Why no?

Is Krishna real? Why is it not the information from scent, touch, voice, taste, and images that returns to the brain and then is perceived? Why not? Why no?

God is a source code, and the character system is the original sin. When the character system is unloaded, the spirit will go back to the source code.

Course 4 relieves one's society persistence. The importance if to relief the persistence, it is not ask one to not to love their family or others. Please do love families and other be loved stuffs.

Course 5

Is image real? Why is it not the information that returns to the brain and then is perceived? Why not? Why no?

Is voice real? Why is it not the information that returns to the brain and then is perceived? Why not? Why no?

Is touch real? Why is it not the information that returns to the brain and then is perceived? Why not? Why no?

Is scent real? Why is it not the information that returns to the brain and then is perceived? Why not? Why no?

Is gustation real? Why is it not the information that returns to the brain and then is perceived? Why not? Why no?

Use the program. See if you can acquire something beyond.

Course 5 relieves one's brain program persistence. All courses requires handwriting or typing for copy the courses. Course 5 ask one to relief the persistence of one's brain program, it is not to ask one to become an idiot. The importance is about persistence but not the brain program themselves.

Course 6

Is belief real? Why is it not the information from scent, touch, voice, and images that returns to the brain and then triggers the program of the brain, or it operates automatically, and then is perceived? Why not? Why no?

Is doubt real? Why is it not the information from scent, touch, voice, taste, and images that returns to the brain and then triggers the program of the brain, or it operates automatically, and then is perceived? Why not? Why no?

Is judgement real? Why is it not the information from scent, touch, voice, taste, and images that returns to the brain and then triggers the program of the brain, or it operates automatically, and then is perceived? Why not? Why no?

Is vanity real? Why is it not the information from scent, touch, voice, taste, and images that returns to the brain and then triggers the program of the brain, or it operates automatically, and then is perceived? Why not? Why no?

Is attempt real? Why is it not the information from scent, touch, voice, taste, and images that returns to the brain and then triggers the program of the brain, or it operates automatically, and then is perceived? Why not? Why no?

Course 6 also requires one to relief the brain program persistence. Brain program contains kinds of forms. Relieving kinds of brain program persistence are similar as removing hairs from a hair bulb.

Course 7

Is time real? Why is it not the information from scent, touch, voice, taste, and images that returns to the brain and then is perceived? Why not? Why no?

Is space real? Why is it not the information from scent, touch, voice, taste, and images that returns to the brain and then is perceived? Why not? Why no?

Is anger real? Why is it not the information from scent, touch, voice, taste, and images that returns to the brain and then triggers the program of the brain, or it operates automatically, and then is perceived? Why not? Why no?

Is thinking real? Why is it not the information from scent, touch, voice, taste, and images that returns to the brain and then triggers the program of the brain, or it operates automatically, and then is perceived? Why not? Why no?

Is calculation real? Why is it not the information from scent, touch, voice, taste, and images that returns to the brain and then triggers the program of the brain, or it operates automatically, and then is perceived? Why not? Why no?

Course 7 requires relieving the space and time persistence. This kind of persistence is information feedback. External information feedback is similar as brain program. External information is comes from other program than one's brain or body.

Course 8

Is daze real? Why is it not the information of scent, touch, voice, taste, and images that returns to the brain and then triggers the program of the brain, or it operates automatically, and then is perceived? Why not? Why no?

Is idea real? Why is it not the information of scent, touch, voice, taste, and images that returns to the brain and then triggers the program of the brain, or it operates automatically, and then is perceived? Why not? Why no?

Is cognizing real? Why is it not the information of scent, touch, voice, taste, and images that returns to the brain and then triggers the program of the brain, or it operates automatically, and then is perceived? Why not? Why no?

Is karma real? Why is it not the information of scent, touch, voice, taste, and images that returns to the brain and then is perceived? Why not? Why no?

Is faith real? Why is it not the information of scent, touch, voice, taste, and images that returns to the brain and then triggers the program of the brain, or it operates automatically, and then is perceived? Why not? Why no?

Course 8 requires relieving conception persistence. Both clear thoughts and

vague thoughts are brain program.

Course 9

Is free will real? Why is it not the information of scent, touch, voice, taste, and images that returns to the brain and then triggers the program of the brain, or it operates automatically, and then is perceived? Why not? Why no?

Is joy real? Why is it not the information of scent, touch, voice, taste, and images that returns to the brain and then triggers the program of the brain, or it operates automatically, and then is perceived? Why not? Why no?

Is distinguishing real? Why is it not the information of scent, touch, voice, taste, and images that returns to the brain and then triggers the program of the brain, or it operates automatically, and then is perceived? Why not? Why no?

Is collective consciousness real? Why is it not the information of scent, touch, voice, taste, and images that returns to the brain and then is perceived? Why not? Why no?

Is material universe real? Why is it not the information of scent, touch, voice, taste, and images that returns to the brain and then is perceived? Why not? Why no?

Course 9 requires relieving the persistence of free will. It is a tricky persistence of one's mind. It is the consciousness makes one to believe the free will. The consciousness of one's mind is also a brain program. Course 9 also requires one to relieving the persistence of one's consciousness. Both consciousness and free will will block the inner peace as well.

Course 10

Is wisdom real? Why is it not the information of scent, touch, voice, taste, and images that returns to the brain and then triggers the program of the brain, or it operates automatically, and then is perceived? Why not? Why no?

Is freedom real? Why is it not the information of scent, touch, voice, taste, and images that returns to the brain and then is perceived? Why not? Why no?

Is evaluating real? Why is it not the information of scent, touch, voice, taste, and images which returns to the brain and then triggers the program of the brain, or it operates automatically, and then is perceived? Why not? Why no?

Is struggle real? Why is it not the information of scent, touch, voice, taste, and images that returns to the brain and then triggers the program of the brain, or it operates automatically, and then is perceived? Why not? Why no?

Is creating real? Why is it not the information of scent, touch, voice, taste, and images that returns to the brain and then triggers the program of the brain, or it operates automatically, and then is perceived? Why not? Why no?

Course 10 requires relieving the persistence of wisdom. It is not to ask one to being stupid but to relieving the persistence. Relieving the persistence of brain program is similar as remove hair from a hair ball. Being patience and precise. The operation automatically such as blood flowing automatically in one's blood vessel is program as well. One's inner part of both body and mind are a small version of universe. And the other program runs automatically outside one's mind and body is the big universe.

Once one acquire the inner peace, the inner peace is the same same the peace of universe. I will use the word Tao to explain it when two kinds of peace are being one.

Course 11

Is logic real? Why is it not the information of scent, touch, voice, taste, and images that returns to the brain and then triggers the program of the brain, or it operates automatically, and then is perceived? Why not? Why no?

Is value real? Why is it not the information of scent, touch, voice, taste, and images that returns to the brain and then is perceived? Why not? Why no?

Is envy real? Why is it not the information of scent, touch, voice, taste, and images that returns to the brain and then triggers the program of the brain, or it operates automatically, and then is perceived? Why not? Why no?

Is operation real? Why is it not the information of scent, touch, voice, taste, and images that returns to the brain and then triggers the program of the brain, or it operates automatically, and then is perceived? Why not? Why no?

Is irritation real? Why is it not the information of scent, touch, voice, taste, and images that returns to the brain and then triggers the program of the brain, or it operates automatically, and then is perceived? Why not? Why no?

Course 11 require relieving the persistence of logic which is also a brain program. Once one relieving almost all persistence of all kinds of programs, it will bring the deepest peace. The inner peace leads to relief.

Course 12

Is boredom real? Why is it not the information of scent, touch, voice, taste, and images that returns to the brain and then triggers the program of the brain, or it operates automatically, and then is perceived? Why not? Why no?

Is aspiration real? Why is it not the information of scent, touch, voice, taste, and images that returns to the brain and then triggers the program of the brain, or it operates automatically, and then is perceived? Why not? Why no?

Is desire real? Why is it not the information of scent, touch, voice, taste, and images that returns to the brain and then triggers the program of the brain, or it operates automatically, and then is perceived? Why not? Why no?

Is comparison real? Why is it not the information of scent, touch, voice, taste, and images that returns to the brain and then triggers the program of the brain, or it operates automatically, and then is perceived? Why not? Why no?

Is wish real? Why is it not the information of scent, touch, voice, taste, and images that returns to the brain and then triggers the program of the brain, or it operates automatically, and then is perceived? Why not? Why no?

These kinds of emotions are also brain programs. Take all programs objectively.

Course 13

Is indifference real? Why is it not the information of scent, touch, voice, taste, and images that returns to the brain and then triggers the program of the brain, or it operates automatically, and then is perceived? Why not? Why no?

Is the outside world real? Why is it not the information of scent, touch, voice, taste, and images that returns to the brain and then is perceived? Why not? Why no?

Are others real? Why is it not the information of scent, touch, voice, taste, and images that returns to the brain and then is perceived? Why not? Why no?

Is pity real? Why is it not the information of scent, touch, voice, taste, and images that returns to the brain and then triggers the program of the brain, or it operates automatically, and then is perceived? Why not? Why no?

Is being thankful real? Why is it not the information of scent, touch, voice, taste, and images that returns to the brain and then triggers the program of the brain, or it operates automatically, and then is perceived? Why not? Why no?

Course 13 relieves from one man's brain and mind upgrade to the bigger programs process. Relieving persistence leads one's small inner peace combining to the bigger peace of universe.

Course 14

Is the past real? Why is it not the information of scent, touch, voice, taste, and images that returns to the brain and then is perceived? Why not? Why no?

Is now real? Why is it not the information of scent, touch, voice, taste, and images that returns to the brain and then is perceived? Why not? Why no?

Is the future real? Why is it not the information of scent, touch, voice, taste, and images that returns to the brain and then is perceived? Why not? Why no?

Is the desire to attack real? Why is it not the information of scent, touch, voice, sense of taste, and images that returns to the brain and then triggers the program of brain, or it operates automatically, and then is perceived? Why not? Why no?

Is desire to control real? Why is it not the information of scent, touch, voice, taste, and images that returns to the brain and then triggers the program of the brain, or it operates automatically, and then is perceived? Why not? Why no?

Course 14 requires one relieves the persistence of time. Time is the universe program. Emotions are perceptual programs, such as desire which is the right side brain program. Male will mostly stuck in the rational program which is the left side brain program. Female needs more attention on the right side brain program, female are mostly stuck in the emotion programs.

After courses of copying by handwriting or typing. Thinking and typing or handwriting by oneself would also be a wisdom option.

Course 15

Is repression real? Why is it not the information of scent, touch, voice, taste, and images that returns to the brain and then triggers the program of the brain, or it operates automatically, and then is perceived? Why not? Why no?

Is sense of honour real? Why is it not the information of scent, touch, voice, taste, and images that returns to the brain and then triggers the program of the brain, or it operates automatically, and then is perceived? Why not? Why no?

Is sense of safety real? Why is it not the information of scent, touch, voice, taste, and images that returns to the brain and then triggers the program of the brain, or it operates automatically, and then is perceived? Why not? Why no?

Is insistence real? Why is it not the information of scent, touch, voice, taste, and images that returns to the brain and then triggers the program of the brain, or it operates automatically, and then is perceived? Why not? Why no?

Is sense of worth real? Why is it not the information of scent, touch, voice, taste, and images that returns to the brain and then triggers the program of the brain, or it operates automatically, and then is perceived? Why not? Why no?

Course 15 requires relieving the persistence of emotion programs. Emotion programs stuck female mostly. Once one female relieving the persistence of several kinds of emotion programs, it leads tremendous peace.

Course 16

Is peace real? Why is it not the information of scent, touch, voice, taste, and images that returns to the brain and then triggers the program of the brain, or it operates automatically, and then is perceived? Why not? Why no?

Is calm real? Why is it not the information of scent, touch, voice, taste, and images that returns to the brain and then triggers the program of the brain, or it operates automatically, and then is perceived? Why not? Why no?

Is inability real? Why is it not the information of scent, touch, voice, taste, and images that returns to the brain and then triggers the program of the brain, or it operates automatically, and then is perceived? Why not? Why no?

Is worry real? Why is it not the information of scent, touch, voice, taste, and images that returns to the brain and then triggers the program of the brain, or it operates automatically, and then is perceived? Why not? Why no?

Is mantra real? Why is it not the information of scent, touch, voice, taste, and images that returns to the brain and then is perceived? Why not? Why no?

After courses of copying by handwriting or typing, it will leads to peace. When one tasted this peace, it also stuck, it will be a new block. And this is the time to letting go the persistence to peace. Course 16 requires relieving the persistence of conceptional programs. Male mostly stuck in rational programs. Conceptional programs mostly stuck males, once male get relieved by conceptional programs, it leads tremendous peace.

Course 17

Is chaos real? Why is it not the information of scent, touch, voice, taste, and images that returns to the brain and then triggers the program of the brain, or it operates automatically, and then is perceived? Why not? Why no?

Is blocking real? Why is it not the information of scent, touch, voice, taste, and images that returns to the brain and then triggers the program of the brain, or it operates automatically, and then is perceived? Why not? Why no?

Is blame real? Why is it not the information of scent, touch, voice, taste, and images that returns to the brain and then triggers the program of the brain, or it operates automatically, and then is perceived? Why not? Why no?

Is sense of guilt real? Why is it not the information of scent, touch, voice, taste, and images that returns to the brain and then triggers the program of the brain, or it operates automatically, and then is perceived? Why not? Why no?

Is the environment real? Why is it not the information of scent, touch, voice, taste, and images that returns to the brain and then is perceived? Why not? Why no?

One beings holds both right side brain and left side brain, males feels world and things more in a left brain way. Females feel world and things more in a right brain way. For one beings, the left side brain logic and way of thinking are the inner male part, the right side brain logic and emotion feelings are inner female part. When one beings get the peace, the second movement requires to balance the rationality and sensibility. It leads a deeper peace. It is a movement to balance the right side brain and left side brain. All courses will slowly upgrade one beings' intelligence. Balancing left side and right side brain also upgrades one beings' intelligence.

Course 18

Is lust real? Why is it not the information of scent, touch, voice, taste, and images that returns to the brain and then triggers the program of the brain, or it operates automatically, and then is perceived? Why not? Why no?

Is love real? Why is it not the information of scent, touch, voice, taste, and images that returns to the brain and then triggers the program of the brain, or it operates automatically, and then is perceived? Why not? Why no?

Is happiness real? Why is it not the information of scent, touch, voice, taste and images that returns to the brain and then triggers the program of the brain, or it operates automatically, and then is perceived? Why not? Why no?

Is sadness real? Why is it not the information of scent, touch, voice, taste, and images that returns to the brain and then triggers the program of the brain, or it operates automatically, and then is perceived? Why not? Why no?

Is beauty real? Why is it not the information of scent, touch, voice, taste, and images that returns to the brain and then is perceived? Why not? Why no?

Course 18 requires relieving the persistence of love and other emotion programs. It is not requires one beings to not to love. The persistence to love is a block to peace and both real love. Same logic, being happy but relieving the persistence to happiness.

Course 19

Is harmony real? Why is it not the information of scent, touch, voice, taste, and images that returns to the brain and then is perceived? Why not? Why no?

Is safeness real? Why is it not the information of scent, touch, voice, taste, and images that returns to the brain and then is perceived? Why not? Why no?

Is danger real? Why is it not the information of scent, touch, voice, taste, and images that returns to the brain and then is perceived? Why not? Why no?

Is acceptance real? Why is it not the information of scent, touch, voice, taste, and images that returns to the brain and then triggers the program of the brain, or it operates automatically, and then is perceived? Why not? Why no?

Is maintenance real? Why is it not the information of scent, touch, voice, taste, and images that returns to the brain and then triggers the program of the brain, or it operates automatically, and then is perceived? Why not? Why no?

Course 19 requires relieving the persistence to harmony. Persistence to harmony is also block the inner peace. It is a tricky persistence. An actual harmony lays already in one's peace which needs no better place or better conditions.

Course 20

Is memory real? Why is it not the information of scent, touch, voice, taste, and images that returns to the brain and then triggers the program of the brain, or it operates automatically, and then is perceived? Why not? Why no?

Is forcing real? Why is it not the information of scent, touch, voice, taste, and images that returns to the brain and then triggers the program of the brain, or it operates automatically, and then is perceived? Why not? Why no?

Is there really a me? Why is it not the information of scent, touch, voice, taste, and images that returns to the brain and then its perceived? Why not? Why no?

Is bashfulness real? Why is it not the information of scent, touch, voice, taste, and images that returns to the brain and then triggers the program of the brain, or it operates automatically, and then is perceived? Why not? Why no?

Is caring real? Why is it not the information of scent, touch, voice, taste, and images that returns to the brain and then triggers the program of the brain, or it operates automatically, and then is perceived? Why not? Why no?

Course 20 requires relieving the persistence to memory. It is not requiring one beings to forget everything, but to relieving the persistence.

Course 21

Is frustration real? Why is it not the information of scent, touch, voice, taste, and images that returns to the brain and then triggers the program of the brain, or it operates automatically, and then is perceived? Why not? Why no?

Is distress real? Why is it not the information of scent, touch, voice, taste, and images that returns to the brain and then triggers the program of the brain, or it operates automatically, and then is perceived? Why not? Why no?

Is the sense of existence real? Why is it not the information of scent, touch, voice, taste, and images that returns to the brain and then triggers the program of the brain, or it operates automatically, and then is perceived? Why not? Why no?

Is premonition real? Why is it not the information of scent, touch, voice, taste, and images that returns to the brain and then triggers the program of the brain, or it operates automatically, and then is perceived? Why not? Why no?

Is respect real? Why is it not the information of scent, touch, voice, taste, and images that returns to the brain and then triggers the program of the brain, or it operates automatically, and then is perceived? Why not? Why no?

Course 21 requires relieving the persistence of emotion programs.

Course 22

Is comfort real? Why is it not the information of scent, touch, voice, taste, and images that returns to the brain and then triggers the program of the brain, or it operates automatically, and then is perceived? Why not? Why no?

Is terror real? Why is it not the information of scent, touch, voice, taste, and images that returns to the brain and then is perceived? Why not? Why no?

Is thirst real? Why is it not the information of scent, touch, voice, taste, and images that returns to the brain and then triggers the program of the brain, or it operates automatically, and then is perceived? Why not? Why no?

Is hunger real? Why is it not the information of scent, touch, voice, taste, and images that returns to the brain and then triggers the program of the brain, or it operates automatically, and then is perceived? Why not? Why no?

Is attention real? Why is it not the information of scent, touch, voice, taste, and images that returns to the brain and then triggers the program of the brain, or it operates automatically, and then is perceived? Why not? Why no?

Course 22 requires relieving the persistence of functional programs.

Course 23

Is selfness real? Why is it not the information of scent, touch, voice, taste, and images that returns to the brain and then triggers the program of the brain, or it operates automatically, and then is perceived? Why not? Why no?

Is selfishness real? Why is it not the information of scent, touch, voice, taste, and images that returns to the brain and then triggers the program of the brain, or it operates automatically, and then is perceived? Why not? Why no?

Is selflessness real? Why is it not the information of scent, touch, voice, taste, and images that returns to the brain and then triggers the program of the brain, or it operates automatically, and then is perceived? Why not? Why no?

Is foolishness real? Why is it not the information of scent, touch, voice, taste, and images that returns to the brain and then triggers the program of the brain, or it operates automatically, and then is perceived? Why not? Why no?

Is clumsiness real? Why is it not the information of scent, touch, voice, taste, and images that returns to the brain and then triggers the program of the brain, or it operates automatically, and then is perceived? Why not? Why no?

Course 23 requires relieving the persistence of programs lays in the consciousness partition programs. To help relief the persistence to consciousness.

Course 24

Is greed real? Why is it not the information of scent, touch, voice, taste, and images that returns to the brain and then triggers the program of the brain, or it operates automatically, and then is perceived? Why not? Why no?

Is sense of going fast real? Why is it not the information of scent, touch, voice, taste, and images that returns to the brain and then triggers the program of the brain, or it operates automatically, and then is perceived? Why not? Why no?

Is sense of going slow real? Why is it not the information of scent, touch, voice, taste, and images that returns to the brain and then triggers the program of the brain, or it operates automatically, and then is perceived? Why not? Why no?

Is differentiation real? Why is it not the information of scent, touch, voice, taste, and images that returns to the brain and then triggers the program of the brain, or it operates automatically, and then is perceived? Why not? Why no?

Is indolence real? Why is it not the information of scent, touch, voice, taste, and images that returns to the brain and then triggers the program of the brain, or it operates automatically, and then is perceived? Why not? Why no?

Course 24 requires relieving a little higher ranks of persistence. Relieving persistence is similar as remove hair from a hair ball, and this is the subtle part of persistence.

Course 25

Is comprehension real? Why is it not the information of scent, touch, voice, taste, and images that returns to the brain and then triggers the program of the brain, or it operates automatically, and then is perceived? Why not? Why no?

Is addiction real? Why is it not the information of scent, touch, voice, taste, and images that returns to the brain and then triggers the program of the brain, or it operates automatically, and then is perceived? Why not? Why no?

Is obsession real? Why is it not the information of scent, touch, voice, taste, and images that returns to the brain and then triggers the program of the brain, or it operates automatically, and then is perceived? Why not? Why no?

Is persecution real? Why is it not the information of scent, touch, voice, taste, and images that returns to the brain and then is perceived? Why not? Why no?

Is awakening real? Why is it not the information of scent, touch, voice, taste, and images that returns to the brain and then triggers the program of the brain, or it operates automatically, and then is perceived? Why not? Why no?

Course 25 requires relieving the persistence to process.

Course 26

Is enlightenment real? Why is it not the information of scent, touch, voice, taste, and images that returns to the brain and then triggers the program of the brain, or it operates automatically, and then is perceived? Why not? Why no?

Is vacancy real? Why is it not the information of scent, touch, voice, taste, and images that returns to the brain and then triggers the program of the brain, or it operates automatically, and then is perceived? Why not? Why no?

Is positivity real? Why is it not the information of scent, touch, voice, taste, and images that returns to the brain and then triggers the program of the brain, or it operates automatically, and then is perceived? Why not? Why no?

Is negativity real? Why is it not the information of scent, touch, voice, taste, and images that returns to the brain and then triggers the program of the brain, or it operates automatically, and then is perceived? Why not? Why no?

Is anxiety real? Why is it not the information of scent, touch, voice, taste, and images that returns to the brain and then triggers the program of the brain, or it operates automatically, and then is perceived? Why not? Why no?

Course 26 requires relieving the persistence of this book itself.

Course 27

Is fluster real? Why is it not the information of scent, touch, voice, taste, and images that returns to the brain and then triggers the program of the brain, or it operates automatically, and then is perceived? Why not? Why no?

Is forwardness real? Why is it not the information of scent, touch, voice, taste, and images that returns to the brain and then triggers the program of the brain, or it operates automatically, and then is perceived? Why not? Why no?

Is separation real? Why is it not the information of scent, touch, voice, taste, and images that returns to the brain and then is perceived? Why not? Why no?

Is encounter real? Why is it not the information of scent, touch, voice, taste, and images that returns to the brain and then is perceived? Why not? Why no?

Is courage real? Why is it not the information of scent, touch, voice, taste, and images that returns to the brain and then triggers the program of the brain, or it operates automatically, and then is perceived? Why not? Why no?

Is confusion real? Why is it not the information of scent, touch, voice, taste, and images that returns to the brain and then triggers the program of the brain, or it operates automatically, and then is perceived? Why not? Why no?

Are these courses real? Why is it not the information of scent, touch, voice, taste, and images that returns to the brain and then is perceived? Why not? Why no?

Is truth real? Why is it not the information of scent, touch, voice, taste, and images that returns to the brain and then is perceived? Why not? Why no?

www.ingramcontent.com/pod-product-compliance
Lightning Source LLC
LaVergne TN
LVHW041551060526
838200LV00037B/1236